Elegies for the
Hot Season

Elegies for the Hot Season

by

SANDRA McPHERSON

Indiana University Press
Bloomington & London

Copyright © 1970 by Indiana University Press

Published in Canada by Fitzhenry & Whiteside Limited, Don Mills, Ontario

Library of Congress catalog number: 79-108214

ISBN: 253-12160-4
Manufactured in the United States of America

For Henry

Contents

1

2

3   *A Season of Change*

4

Acknowledgments

The author gratefully acknowledges permission from the publishers to reprint the following poems which have appeared previously: "Deus Ex Machina," in *Perspective;* "The Tax Assessor," in *Kayak;* "Preparation," in *The Colorado Quarterly;* "Worlds of Different Sizes," in *The Nation;* "Peace Talks" and "Foetal Pig," in *Shenandoah;* "Paper Snake," in *Puget Soundings;* "Trout" and "Labor," in *The Quest;* "In the Columbia River Gorge," in *Quixote;* "Resigning from a Job in a Defense Industry" and "Amanitas," in *Field;* "Lions," in *The Carleton Miscellany;* "While You're Gone," in *Choice;* "Selling the House," "All You Need," "Keeping House," "Balm," "Succeeding a Fraternity into an Old House," "On the Move," and "A Gift of Trilliums," in *Northwest Review;* "Lake and Moon: Two Versions of Death," "View from Observatory Hill," "Roof Rat," "The Plant," "Losing Ground," "Elegies for the Hot Season," "You, Asleep," "Pisces Child," and "Evolving an Instinct," in *Poetry Northwest;* and "His Body," © 1970 and "Autumnal," © 1969 by the Modern Poetry Association, in *Poetry.* "View from Observatory Hill" also appeared in Borestone Mountain Awards' *Best Poems of 1968.* "Lions" owes a few lines to George B. Schaller's "Life with the King of Beasts" in *National Geographic.*

1

Lake and Moon: Two Versions of Death

They don't fit me, either one, like a dress too big.
I thought once the moon was a fragrant onion,
And the lake its cyclopean teardrop.
But they are big and impersonal as a corporation.
They have ruled, No Weeping.

No more do deer and willows drink at the lake-edge.
I will not set foot in it,
For it is a moat, and no one crosses it
Alive. Drop after drop has disappeared in it,
Smothered.

And the moon is no longer the warm woman she was.
She is fruitless, she grows fat, like a spayed bitch.
She strikes the lake, she is a willful wife.
She offers me her leaden pillow,
I have never slept well on it.

I am a coin these merchants flip. Mr. Lake, the inexhaustible,
If he wins, won't swallow, he will dissolve.
And the moon every day like a clock-hand
Chalks me a round grave. Tonight the moon
Has risen red as a dead

Camellia. She makes a wound
On the lake. Soon she will turn again death-pale.
They are too big, they have the vote and the rule.
Between them the deer and the willows and I, not yet
    shadows,
Move. Between, a tugboat

Beats its heart out.

Poppies

Orange is the single-hearted color. I remember
How I found them in a vein beside the railroad,
A bumble-bee fumbling for a foothold
While the poppies' petals flagged beneath his boot.

I brought three poppies home and two buds still sheathed.
I amputated them above the root. They lived on artlessly
Beside the window for a while, blazing orange, bearing me
No malice. Each four-fanned surface opened

To the light. They were bright as any orange grove.
I watched them day and night stretch open and tuck shut
With no roots to grip, like laboratory frogs' legs twitching
Or like red beheaded hens still hopping on sheer nerves.

On the third afternoon one bud tore off its green glove
And burst out brazen as Baby New Year.
Two other poppies dropped their petals, leaving four
Scribbly yellow streamers on a purple-brimmed and green

Conical cadaver like a New Year's hat.
I'd meant to celebrate with them, but they seemed
So suddenly tired, these aging ladies in crocheted
Shawl leaves. They'd once been golden as the streets

Of heaven, now they were as hollow.
They couldn't pull together for a last good-bye.
I had outlived them and had only their letters to read,
Fallen around the vase, saying they were sorry.

View from Observatory Hill

It looks to me like a clock shop window,
Time-faces, no two set alike, swearing each one
By its different hour. I lost trust in my bedside clock
Long ago when its two black eyebrows frowned irate
At ten of two, turned worried at three forty-five.
Stars can't be so faithless.

They seem most intimate with space, that man
Who has everything. Perhaps one is even
His bellybutton jewel; others seem to be stars
In his crown. But I'm sure they are intimates and of high caste.
Days they want complete privacy.

So tonight I've climbed to this wild mustard-covered,
Knee-shaped hill of our mother earth, while the domeroof
    draws
Its curtain back, and, voyeur of all,
The telescope swings round, gets comfortable to peer.

Lightyears arrive thick as vacationers to camp
In my eye. They're not people of leisure and their stay
Is short. I'm not so gregarious I would return
The call. Stars are strewn like caltrops all over space.
I easily get lost.

Days they watch me through a one-way
Mirror. Nights I try to talk direct,
Sweating off worry, awe, and wishes to them, my pulse
Flashing through its tunnels in the wave-length
I do best. Squinting, still the stars can't read me.

With communications out, they tease for war.
Like any crowd they start by nudging, shoving,

Happy-handed as a lynching mob. Then one star
Rides away like the hangman's horse, circles
In a nooselike orbit. Sweeping me off my feet one day,
He chops me down the next.

Space caves in about me like a mineshaft.
I find some stars that I believe in hang there dead.
I see that heaven is a place of fires like hell.
I know that light is relentless and has no language,
That where I live, light long since coughed dead out.

Insects oscillate in the field of wild mustard,
Wings lathery in the starlight. It may be stars
Light up in delight, for some unknowable plum
That made their day, like mockingbirds at midnight singing,
Like someone smiling in his sleep.

Roof Rat

When the palm was green and innocent, she kept you,
Much evicted tenant, escapee from poisoned gardens.
You came packing gifts like your own Santa Claus.
Hidden like a louse in her thick wig, you set up

Laboratory, home, and pyre, building a shelter
That would commit your life like a wedding ring.
The palm's long fingers could not pry into that privacy,
Not even the sky could bully you. One day,

With the relish of an antiquary, you carried to your nest
A shard of glass, revolving it like a flower arrangement
To find the best angle, letting the light crawl bare-
Wristed and unshoed across its little furnace. I watched

You come and go, soloing along the telephone cables,
Digging your nails into the shredding shingles of the palm
    trunk,
Flicking your whiskers against its whiskers. You built
As one possessed, belonging to no union. And though I lived

Across the street, you would have none of me, rat
Aristocrat, penthouse Pete. Then one day the sun
Bore a small twin of itself
On the other side of the glass. The palm

Became a blonde and then a torch of liberty.
I heard your crackling laughter at the firetruck's
Red rescue, its hoses sniping at your homemade star,
The nova of your rodent's heaven, your tree landlady

Dumb with illumination. You burned like God in the wilder-
    ness
Bush. We stood a mass of Moseses, lifting our feet
On the hot street. And you burned, untouchable
In the locked house of fire, and the light in our eyes was you.

Deus Ex Machina

I

What does he offer me, this angel
  Of appliances?
Straight from his oven heaven,
  He peddles
Comfort, weeping counsellors
  Of ice or iron,
Hot or cold piped to the blood.
  He is
So serviceable, his temperament
  So tepid.

He sells disposals, guaranteed. Nothing
  Lives long
In a kitchen, in this secondary
  Slaughter house.
Scraps are exiled. Mouths
  Are drunk
Away. I look for friends in the fragments.
  He
Signs an X, escaping like steam.
  I see
Him hawking
  Over
Me.

II

I have gone to the laundromat, love,
To the coin slots, to the windows.

I have gone to hear the silver pinched,
To see the white shirts tossing,

To see the movies on the drums, to hear
The folded towels wheeled in wire baskets.

Sleeves and cuffs I see, sleeves
And cuffs, and buttons hard as rose-thorns.

I have gone between the blue and orange
Boxes for the show, for searching dryers—

Clear as bald men's eyes—for lint,
For the double load, for the eclipse.

Selling the House

Nothing of ours there now. Nothing to comfort, nothing to
    break.
The bedrooms stretch and yawn off the dining room. The
    kitchen
Goes hungry. The bathrooms remain unnecessary complica-
    tions
In the emptiness.

Everything's clean as a cloud,

But who's fooled? Not the faucets drooping forlorn
As willows over a dry stream bed. Not the dumbwaiter,
Trapped in the basement, a damned soul: dust
The gypsy lives there.

Must have shocked the old place

When we moved in, splashing color on the floor, dropping
Our fat sofas, fat people dropping onto them. We slapped
Pictures on its walls like band-aids. We brought our own light
Like missionaries.

Sold. Sold out. The roof

Will have no more temptation to eavesdrop;
The basement, no reason to sweep back its shadows.
The steps needn't be servants any more:
Sky walks them.

Nobody needs you now, house,

But nobody leaves you alone. Mounted on your
Sunken pedestal, nailed down with marigolds, you'll fall

Against our ears and wishes. We'll see
Our past

For the awkward lumber it is.

Then that goes too.
They say that it's easy,
Merely an erasure,
Quick as tomorrow,

Simple as forgiving.

The Plant

If it came to change our lives, it didn't want
Step-forward converts. And if we were
Hamhanded or clayfooted when it came,
We weren't healed. It rode our straight days
On a merry-go-round, chinked our aimless hours

On its keyring. Rarefied, lanky,
Stunning as a man back from the dead,
It drew in birdsongs, housewives' chatter. Dogs howled
Into it; men felt small by it. And all the time its face
Remained unmoved as a psychiatrist's.

Rising from its broad platform leaves,
Face tranced on the moon, mopping the wet wind
In storms, blossoming, its blossoming
A coronation, the plant was not one of us but a gift
Of itself. It suffered our stares until

It died, blurring like a UFO, never geysering
In our air again. The wonder gone,
Our lives shambled apart. We were the audience
After a play, agreeing no more together
What to laugh at, when to cry.

Losing Ground

Our lawn bent to the corner like a boomerang.
We trusted its even temper, its clan loyalty.
That lawn was a norm, it was our equator,
Our sea-level.

A brand-new house showed all our wares,
All we were: one story; no attic, no basement
Sorting our past into good dreams
And nightmares.

Seventy-five houses huddled on this old
Grazing-land, our home covering the ranch-house site.
And then we saw the dip, a ladle shape, in the center
Of our comfort,

Easing downward, a perfect circle on the lawn.
Just a dimple, we thought, or our personal valley.
But if there were a drouth we knew where to dig.
We felt our well's

Tugging like divining rods. Soon we could hide
Where we'd stood before, competing
With the trees. Only a landscape worry: we filled
The depression

Till we made a mound. An Easter hat
Of pink and white flowers resurrects there
Each spring. But the ground it grows on
Is sinking.

Always, before, the water we trusted came
Out of open sky; when it welled
From our own clay we begged for temperance.
We stoppered

That gift bottle opening itself. But the current
Flowed, still flows. There is a sliding bottom
We cannot see. Land drowns by its own
Undertow.

Once more our hillock slips into a cup saying "Drink."
We feed it mud each year. If you are thirsty
Don't come to our well. It's a long fall.
It will take all your life.

Elegies for the Hot Season

1. *The Killing of the Snails*
Half the year has hot nights, like this,
When gnats fly thick as stars, when the temperature is taken
On the tongues of flowers and lovers,
When the just-dead is buried in warm sod.
The snail-pebbled lawns glimmer with slime trails, and the un-
   worried,
Unhurried snail tucks into his dark knuckle, stockaded
With spears of grass, safe. When I first heard
The sound of his dying, it was like knuckles cracking.

The lightest foot can slay snails. Their shells break
More easily than mirrors. And like bad luck, like
A face in a mirror, they always come back.

Good hunting nights were stuffy as a closed room.
No moon shone but my father's flashlight.
As if it were Jericho, he circled the house,
And I'd hear all evening the thick crunch
Of his marching, the sound of death due
To his size 13 shoe.

In the morning I'd find them, little clots on the grass, pretend
They'd been singed by geranium fire-bursts, asphyxiated by
   blue
Iris flame, burnt to shadows under the strawberry blossom.
The fuchsias bled for them. White-throated calla lilies
Maintained appearances above the snail slum.

But the slow-brained pests forgave and fragilely claimed the
   garden
The next hot season, like old friends, or avengers.

2. *The Killing of the Caterpillars*

Today I watch our neighbor celebrating May,
Ringing round the besieged cherry-tree,
His haunted maypole, brandishing his arson's torch
Through the tents of caterpillars. He plays conductor,
Striking his baton for the May music.
And the soft, fingery caterpillars perform,
Snap, crackle, pop.

They plummet through a holiday of leaves like fireworks or
    shooting stars or votive candles
Or buttercups, under the hex of the neighbor's wand, first
    fruits of euthanasia,
Ripe and red before the cherries. And it is over,
Grown cold as a sunset. They lie on the grass
Still and black as those who lie under it.

It is night. Lights burn in the city
Like lamps of a search-party, like the search-beam
Of my father's flashlight, at every swing discovering
Death.

2

The Tax Assessor

Money goes smiling from one man to another,
A woman. The assessor's black suit

Grimaces front and back as he walks.
His mouth is a number ten turned edgewise

Like a brand. He looks only at the sides
Of buildings. He looks pale. In the garden

His shoeprints dig shallow graves.
From his groin pocket shoots a tapemeasure

Of spring steel. His girl's statistics: thirty
By fifty by forty-five feet. Our shadows

Cross, cling like two mourners. Why should I
Fear him? He says I am worth something.

Preparation

It was likely to occur during the happiest story
Or at the explosion of a brainstorm or as the product fused
From mere numbers. The blue sky we knew would go
Yellow and fearsick, then after the flash, white

As a bloodless Caucasian. What we had to learn was like danc-
    ing:
To follow. A desk, no protection from the teacher's C,
Would save our lives. There were times we wondered—would
    we
Go all at once, tightly curled little foetuses, roomsful

Of legal abortions? A brace of peace
Holding our shoulders back bent. We were suspicious
Of white dawns. We kept one ear ready always
For the voice of our siren mother.

We expect now the friendly alarm Wednesdays
As Sunday we depend on brimstone to quake the church.
Some say that God alone, though he doesn't laugh, is not
    scared. And that
There still are those who sing without government like birds

And are prepared.

Resigning from a Job in a Defense Industry

The names of things—sparks!
I ran on them like a component:
Henries, microhenries, Blue
Beavers, wee wee ductors:
Biographer of small lives,
Of a plug and his girl named Jack,
Of Utopian colonies which worked—
Steel, germanium, brass, aluminum,
Replaceables.
                    Outside, afloat, my words
Swung an arm charting the woman
Who was the river bottom.

We tried, beyond work, at work,
To keep what we loved. Near
Christmas I remember the office
Women trimming their desperately
Glittering holy day trees. And,
Just as I left, the company
Talent show, the oils and sentiment
Thick on still lifes and seacoasts,
The brush strokes tortured as a child's
First script. Someone
Had studied driftwood; another man,
The spray of a wave, the mania
Of waters above torpedoes.

Peace Talks

"A peasant trick"—whatever
Goes wrong blame weather—everything
Coming right, things
And weather, waits for us
In the back of the brain like a chair.

In the midst, on the other hand,
Of a favorite season we allow
Ourselves greater pain thinking
The leaves will carry us—
A gambler's trick.

But there are agreements
With the weather not often entered
Into otherwise—given, say, a Santa
Ana hot wind or a hurricane—
Such as surrender.

Amanitas

For a still life we pick them, above the beach
Between polished kinnikinnick and the brow

Of the wood's edge. Sploshes of rain roll off our boots
And arms. The mushrooms advertise—

Yellow-slickered, orange warning Wet Paint if not
Caution, warted and Christmas knicknack

Red. Their youngsters stick up gross big toes.
Worms patrolling the heliotrope corals

Set no foot in these. O we are deadly. Our brown
Bags eat them up, certain of their fertility

And new night-fruit. Home we litter indoors
With the outdoor—sand, rain, grass and what

Will still pose for life in the muscarias.
The mycelium squirms sub-visible. You can tell

Centuries later a dead-of-mushrooms mummy—the pinched
Nose, the unbearable skin over pain, pain

A growing thing with a season and a harvest.
There is no uprooting it. Or perhaps these make

Ezekiels with visions a Russian Korjak will trade
A reindeer for. His cup runneth over even unto

The urine, which he will drink, which intoxicates.
I trade only the emptiness of my hands

And eyes for this modern and American generation
That mockingly doffs its enamelled cap and which

I love for its fight for my heart
And which I must fight to love.

Worlds of Different Sizes

I like to help small things survive:
Red slugs drying on sidewalk deserts,
Birds against cats, cats against dogs, dogs against cars.

I like to help big things keep going:
Old trees, three-story houses,
Mountains ore-men want to dig away.

And the invisible, the invisible, how it struggles
For its life in big blind bones,
In a small heart.

Foetal Pig

When I cut through
Beyond all requirements,
Snapped off nose,
Snipped a quick canal through the eyes,
To enter that brain,
I stood where whole ages
Of new birth were needed
To bring such a pig to me again:

One I could hold, black and red
Like old lipstick and sequins,
Which was a little me
Without my luck, and in
The empty flower pot cells of
Whose brain were planted
The scissors of the merely curious.

Paper Snake

A paper snake,
A two-dime, white, black, and bean-brown snake from Hong
  Kong
Tempted me to buy. It was flawed
But therein our rapport.
Windowy, concertinaed lengths between thirteen
Spots
Wavy as shadows on water, its body
Curves with a replica of that curve
In its tongue.
All its flightiness centers there
In the two smoky bird-feather barbs of the tongue, for
Its body proper rides the verge
Between ground and that medium of fancy and light,
Of which it may know but little,
Its tail
Indicating backwards and the clay
Head made blunt—unnecessarily—as
A heel (it's not
A Christian snake):
It is elastic as all possibilities
Of imperfection.

Trout

The jonquil yellow of our apartment wears a flat hat
Green as a bruise. A storm grays up this day you

Finally go fishing but breaks for one moment of sun
On a white clapboard house before sunset. Home,

Wading in shadows, I imagine your fish story. All
Week you've tied May flies and streamers and gaudy

Salmon flies whose breathing counterparts have such
Big eyes you can't hook them for bait. The garden

Of the clapboard house has suggested a color scheme
For our livingroom—blue, lavender and white,

Magenta briefly, one red-orange oriental poppy and
A few wild golden poppies just peering over the grass.

In an hour the brilliant flowers will be flayed,
Their stems rot black, and my whole view be razed to

An even evil temper. That is the current we go with.
The sunny ephemerids did not hatch. The trout

Eluded you, melding their golden, brown and rainbow
Watercolor tints to black, flicking their smile

Like a spark out of mind. Your eyes hook west and you
Headlight home like a late sun down the last garden

Avenue of hues, toward colors the living shore up
In their livingrooms, and leave night's black,

No color at all, to have its day.

In the Columbia River Gorge, After a Death

These only wait—

Red apples, thronged
Mouths, whole dumb
Choirs of them—

Tall cliffs, blue,
Shadowy,
Haughty chins.

They are the fathers
Of their own
Feet

Wading below,
Taking forever
To be carved.

And then
What can they expect?
This is patient country.

Like the river, I should leave here.
I should be home in sorrow with you.
Yet this landscape

Shows me
How he died, how he became suddenly
No more man

But that unseizable
Cleaving
Edge the patient expect.

Even my child,
That first blood shed,
Awake in the hospital nursery,

Born and more
Herself than she will ever be,
Lives only at the mercy

Of cloud and cliff-edge,
Under that weathercock mercy,
My little waterfall.

When I come too close,
Earth shuts up its tongues,
But I hear what it means

In the idling motor, in the note
Child-held until the breath runs out,
In the unwinding

Music of the spawning fish,
Playing against the current
Into some longsuffering water.

Land, if I take you
Into my fist,
There

You'll stay, longer than I can hold you,
So patient you are,
Waiting

At the end of the breadline
For your loaf
Of ash,

Of flesh.

Lions

Lions don't need your help. In the Serengeti,
For instance, one thousand like the very rich

Hold sway over more than Connecticut. The mane
Of the lion, like the hooked jaw of the male salmon,

Acts as a shield for defense and is the gift
Of sexual selection. His eyes are fathomless amber.

The lion is the most social of the big cats.
Pride members are affectionate among themselves.

They rub cheeks when they meet. They rest
And hunt together. And cubs suckle indiscriminately.

But strangers or members of a neighboring pride are not
Usually accepted. If a pride male meets a strange female

He may greet her in a friendly fashion
And even mate with her

But the pride females will drive her off.
Male lions, usually depicted as indolent freeloaders

Who let the lionesses do all the hunting, are not mere
Parasites. They maintain the integrity of the territory.

Lions eat communally but completely lack table manners.
Indeed, lions give the impression that their evolution

Toward a social existence is incomplete—that cooperation
In achieving a task does not yet include

The equal division of the spoils.
More bad news: lions are not good parents.

But prowess, that they have. Their courage comes
From being built, like an automobile,

For power. A visible lion is usually a safe lion,
But one should never feel safe

Because almost always there is something one can't see.
Given protection and power

A lion does not need to be clever.
Now, lions are not the most likable kind of animal

Unless you are a certain type of person,
That is, not necessarily leonine in the sense of manly

Or ferocious, but one who wouldn't mind resting twenty
Of twenty-four hours a day and who is not beyond

Stealing someone else's kill
About half the time.

Lions are not my favorite kind of animal,
Gazelles seem nicer,

A zebra has his own sort of appealing pathos,
Especially when he is sure prey for the lion.

Lions have little to offer the spirit.
If we made of ourselves parks and placed the lion

In the constituent he most resembled
He would be in our blood.

3

A Season of Change

All You Need

Gooseflesh plaster walls
We live between
With a mirror like a giant
Snail trail down one wall—

It is all you need,
Somewhere to look, to turn
Away from, somewhere you can't
See yourself.

And a broad window
With screens, like peanut-
Butter jars we kept caterpillars
In on leaves, holes

Punched in the lid. For air.
For an air yielding
Like a woman to sweep our cells
And buoy

Up the blood
Keeping our skin house hot
Between chilly walls,
Between chills.

Keeping House

I never intended this.
Just a house clean, sharp as a knife.
None of this poltergeist
Leaking and cracking and smudging, not

The silver mink
Mildew fuzzing the window frame,
Electric cords ribbon-
Worming behind the phonograph. Bolshevik

Insects insist
We share space, squat
In corners previously bare, strain
Through screens,

Warm on the hot plates
Of windows. Around the ceiling
Our isolate spider runs
Like a train.

So spring breaks—breaks in!
The walls crawl
Where cellophane light blinks
Among shadows

Of willow leaves bursting their buds.
Honey-pot ants decorate the pane
Like ankhs a pyramid.
They are brimful.

The house is brimful.
Eden, pure Eden is chasing us.
The baby is pounding her bars
To get out.

Balm

Like a skeleton, the old woman who has kept
Herself in shape suns by the pool. Gray, gouged cat
Hair skids from last evening's spat.
I spring-clean and hem thin
Dresses, flags, alibis. The baby gets away
With what she can.

These hours are such a balm. Our voices ring
Bright, they hold in their rain. Gardening
On a whim, you attack Jack's
Beanstalk weeds with a crowbar. Tap, tap, tap,
The needle tests—a blind man—
For my thumb.

Holy or not, we fatten like lambs
In this city of refuge, this day of rest. The old
Woman occults. Paper
Wasps in the eaves swing their hovering
Hotel, their doors by ours wide open.
—Pax, pax, your skull-bare

Garden smiles, my work's gone underground.

Succeeding a Fraternity into an Old House

The facade is turquoise,
Set in the silver sky
Like a garish Navajo brooch,
Bigger than beauty.

Inside it's clear the old
Tenants hold no idea
Of vacancy.
They refuse to permit

The solitude of a house,
A space,
A time between people. For us
They leave bottles

With no messages,
Rat-dark shoes,
Oven crusty with offerings
To the gods, basin

Numbering their hairs.
Who so poor
Needs to inherit these?
Footloose

Dust wins the shoes,
A witch the hair. The rest
Bumps with its raw
Companions to the dump.

Goodbye, beer bottle,
Urn of conscience. Goodbye,
Beds, sallow
And limp. The oak

Floor creaks: we'll make
It shine. We'll paint
The walls saint-white.
This will be our next heaven.

On the Move

Town to country to town again we're on the move.
Your shirts are packed like a kill of ducks, my fox
Hat bristles at its cage. For a month
We're strong as coolies paid the wages of our possessions.

To look at painful as a sunburn this wallpaper
Must peel. The porch sags,
Lap sat on too long. In the basement a black
Widow fights for your hand and squatter's rights.

We're the new government. The patria we rent.
Your suits fly loyally in and out of the door.
We keep a wilderness in adytum,
Den, scriptorium. The walls we tax with paintings.

Cat-eyed, the baby whets
Her nails on the plaster. She'll tame—
In time to move out, move on, packing these bodies
We home in and hers, the tiny, only house we've built.

A Gift of Trilliums

Bandage-white and healthy
Illegally they came
From their wild bed in the ferns
To our back door. You saw them
Far off and ran
To dig your fingers around roots
Frailer than baby hands,
To baby the two heads,
Siamese on one root, home
To this human mother.

Nurse, the spade!—the kitchen
Spoon. Our first transplant
Flops completely: one stalk's
A collapsing lung, the other,
Face in the mud, prays
For our disgrace.
They are just out of breath.
They need an Easter and lo,
Three days healing, they do
Spring back, show
Their napkin-white faces,
Come blushing into being.

It is their new life which is
Your gift, not their old wood-
Wild prettiness
And privacy: this new
Prosperity they shout like lepers
Lucky to be healed.
Among the snow-browned shrubs and
Dandelions of our rented garden
These trilliums stun

Like nudes, though you knew
Not how they would bless when you
Thieved them nor did I know
How like our flesh they would become.

4

Pregnancy

It is the best thing.
I should always like to be pregnant,

Tummy thickening like a yoghurt,
Unbelievable flower.

A queen is always pregnant with her country.
Sheba of questions

Or briny siren
At her difficult passage,

One is the mountain that moves
Toward the earliest gods.

Who started this?
An axis, a quake, a perimeter,

I have no decisions to master
That could change my frame

Or honor.
Immaculate. Or if it was not, perfect.

Pregnant, I'm highly explosive—
You can feel it, long before

Your seed will run back to hug you—
Squaring and cubing

Into reckless bones, bouncing odd ways
Like a football.

The heart sloshes through the microphone
Like falls in a box canyon.

The queen's only a figurehead.
Nine months pulled by nine

Planets, the moon slooping
Through its amnion sea,

Trapped, stone-mad . . . and three
Beings' lives gel in my womb.

While You're Gone

Trillium and
Apple blossom
I sit in—your

Clean underthings,
Cotton breastplates,
Tail-ends

Of you. I pick
One up,
It snaps!

It's lived with you
Long enough,
Has your

Spark
And shock,
Your last word.

They're all so feverish.
They're spring
Fluffing out each

Week for you.
My spider, they're webs
Of you.

Smothered in them
I'm
Again bride-white.

They cling to my face.

You, Asleep

You're off again, Jonah, on your wild ride.
Your fish takes you away
Beyond harbor, beyond day,
Into the moon's pull.

He brings you into the belly of errors
Stinking despite burial in their thin membranes,
Contorting the flower's message:
Forget me not. He draws you

Into the spewing up of memory, says
You must serve the old
In their presumption to live. You must pay
For the over-preserved whom you want to die.

And this God-sent insatiable,
Does he take you for old sin?
Does he need you? Even like you? Tonight
What has he prepared to spur your endless and slow conver-
    sion?

O put out your hand,
White as a shell,
So that I may know
You are undrowned

And are not come back self-sick,
But are back. What is there to do with this fish,
This moon's pet on the moon's leash?
Who can catch him?

Labor

"You'll forget about it,"
I didn't want to,

Pupil in the white of an eye,
Only thing that could see.

The starving of Leningrad
Shrank back and forth on the pavement

Three stories down; in her Demerol
Pond the fish slowed.

Awake! awake! awake!
And when I'm not it's babble

Or a rabbit nose,
Everyone's normal case.

My belly's an old hill in childhood.
To think of the texture

Of anything else—an oak leaf,
Sand—it's impossible.

Little bullet,
Come out, come out!

I've a slim dress to wear,
I've a joy.

Pisces Child

Those calm swamp-green eyes,
Gliding like alligators,
Float to this shore
And bump awake.

Sea-legs jerk.
Hands swim still, submarine pink, the palms
Stretched out like starfish.
I'm the old wharf you live on.

Your tongue draws oceans in, not spitting
A word out. Quick, fluttery, slight
As a guppy,
Coercive as undertow.

Oh paramecium
I am your gross-pored mama. Hydra,
An elephant
Suckles you.

In the wilderness you are a spring.
You perpetually melt,
Lake and river maker, dedicated as the porpoise
To return to the sea.

Do you want both worlds?
I see you rooting,
Arms random, then possessive, like potatoes
Sprouting.

Or, needing, needing to need,
You cry yourself purple as eggplant.
You are wordless, but never mind:
You have your sort of song.